ART DECO
SPOT ILLUSTRATIONS AND MOTIFS
513 ORIGINAL DESIGNS

BY WILLIAM ROWE

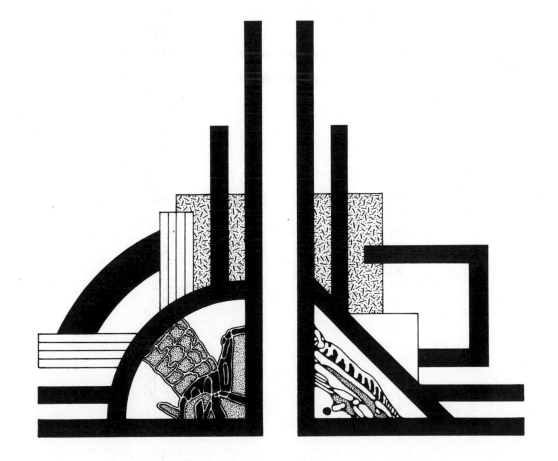

DOVER PUBLICATIONS INC., NEW YORK

PUBLISHER'S NOTE

The designs presented on these pages are William Rowe's latest interpretations of Art Deco, a style into which he has breathed new life. As in previous volumes (*Original Art Deco Designs*, 22567-4; *New Art Deco Borders and Motifs*, 24709-0), the artist incorporates stylized themes taken from nature into designs rendered with a masterly control of black and white. The results are capable of almost infinite adaptation: Portions can be added or omitted, according to need and preference; the central sections of many motifs, left empty, can be filled with elements of appropriate shape that Mr. Rowe has provided.

Copyright © 1985 by Dover Publications, Inc.
All rights reserved under Pan American and International Copyright Conventions.

Published in Canada by General Publishing Company, Ltd., 30 Lesmill Road, Don Mills, Toronto, Ontario.
Published in the United Kingdom by Constable and Company, Ltd.

Art Deco Spot Illustrations and Motifs: 513 Original Designs is a new work, first published by Dover Publications, Inc., in 1985.

DOVER *Pictorial Archive* SERIES

Manufactured in the United States of America
Dover Publications, Inc., 31 East 2nd Street, Mineola, N.Y. 11501

Library of Congress Cataloging in Publication Data

Rowe, William, 1946–
    Art Deco spot illustrations and motifs.

    (Dover pictorial archive series)
    1. Art deco—Themes, motives. 2. Decoration and ornament—History—20th century—Themes, motives. I. Title. II. Series.
NK1396.A76R67 1985   745.4'4924   85-6843
ISBN 0-486-24924-7 (pbk.)

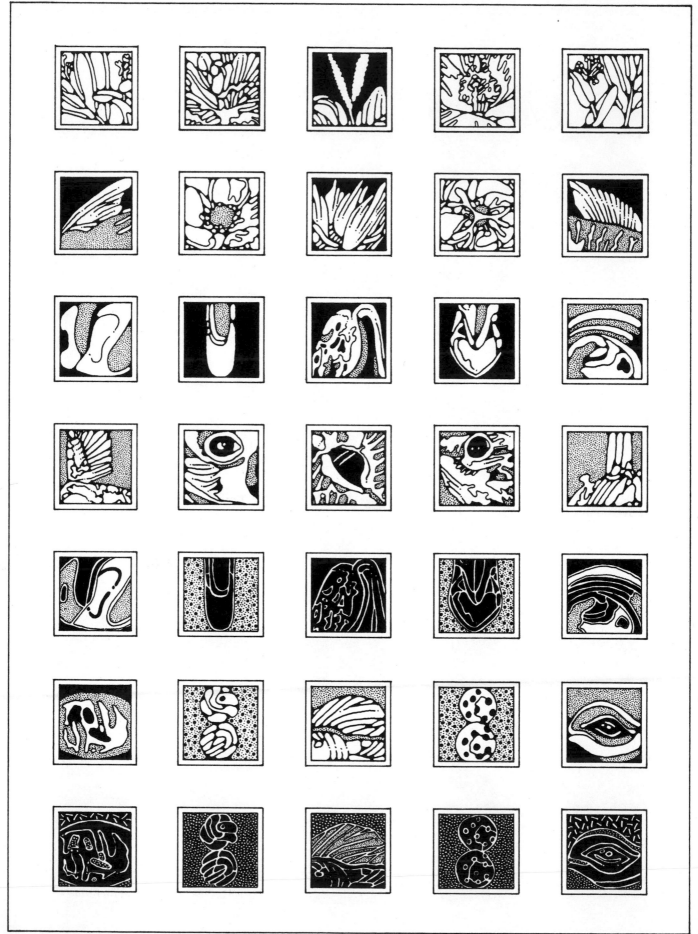

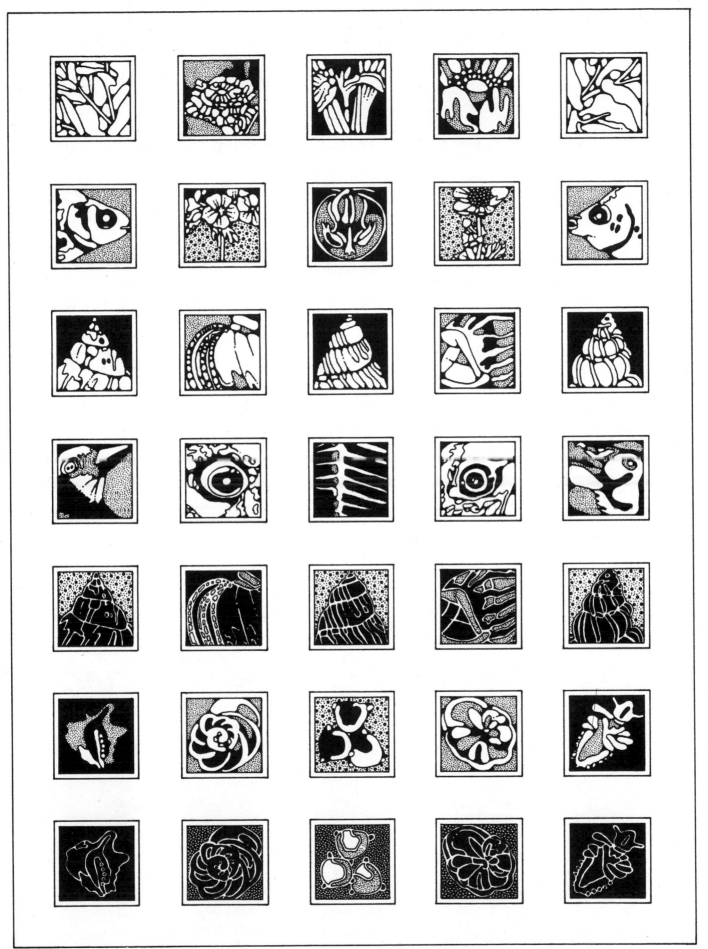

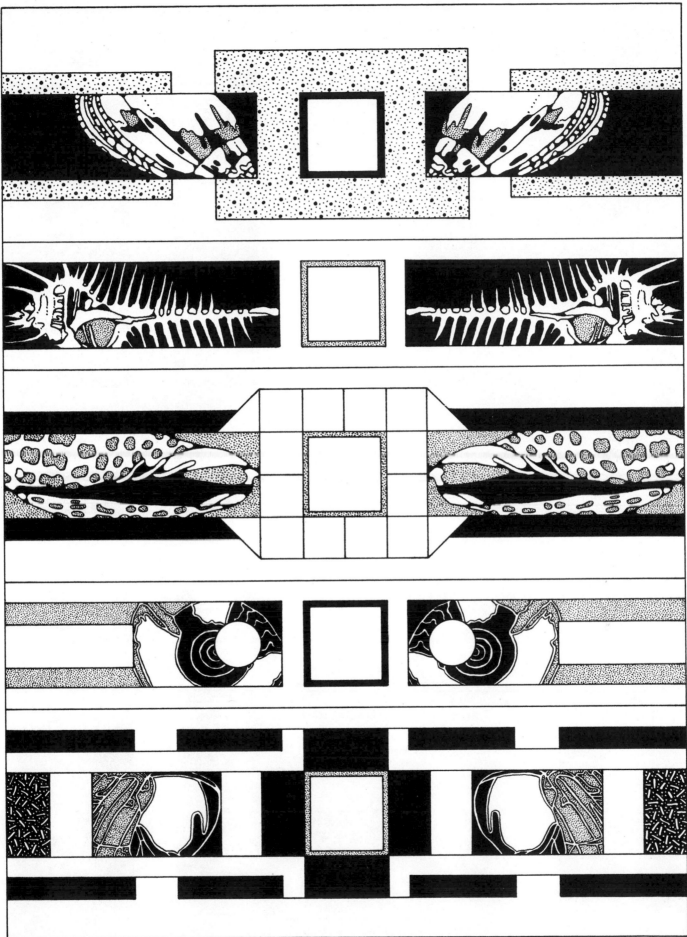

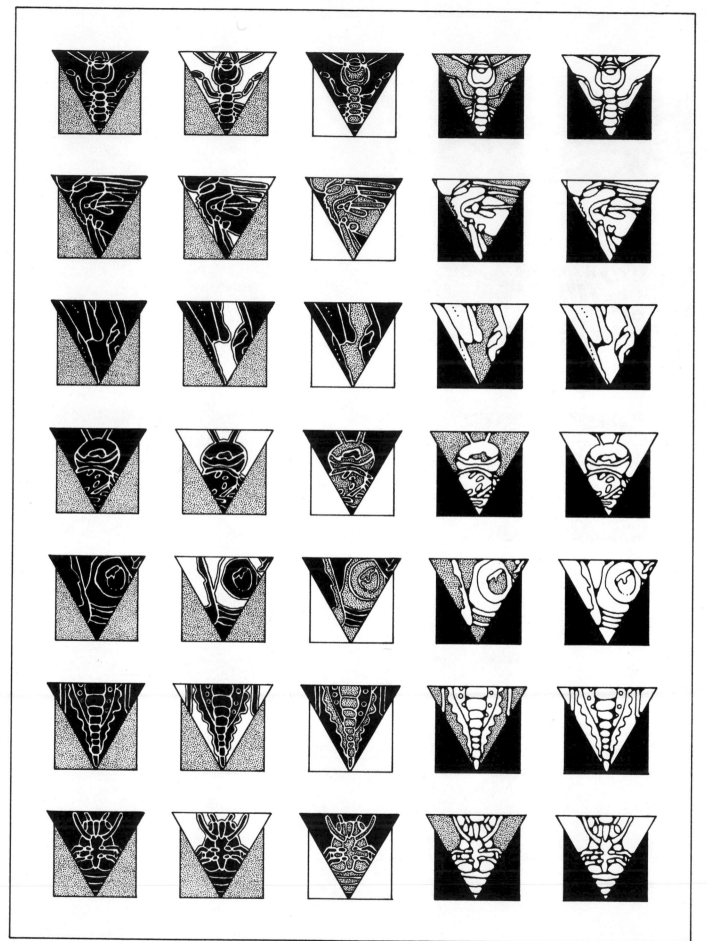

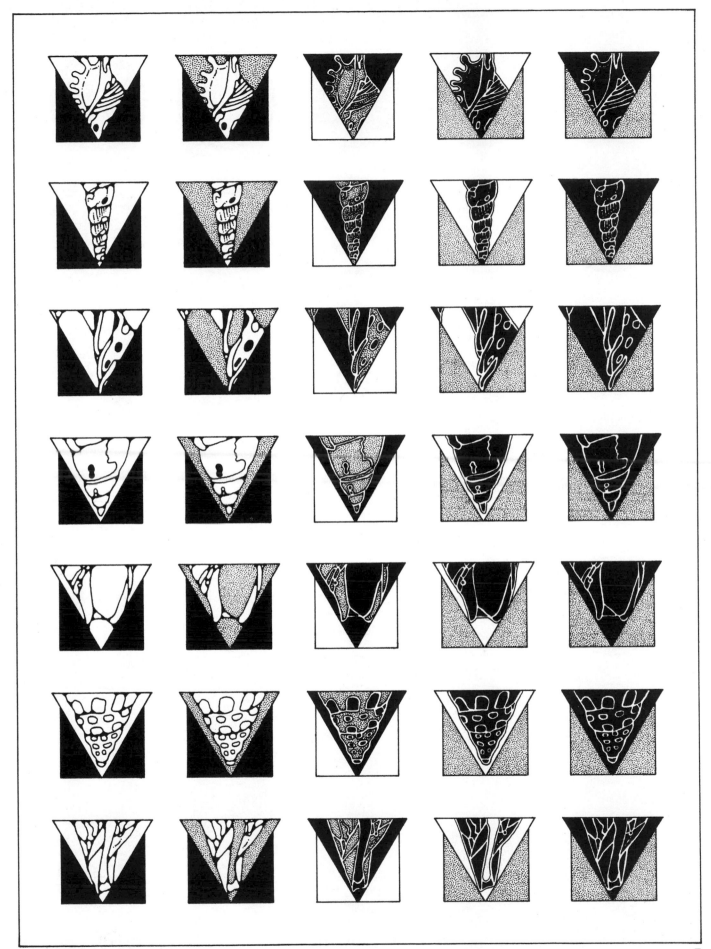

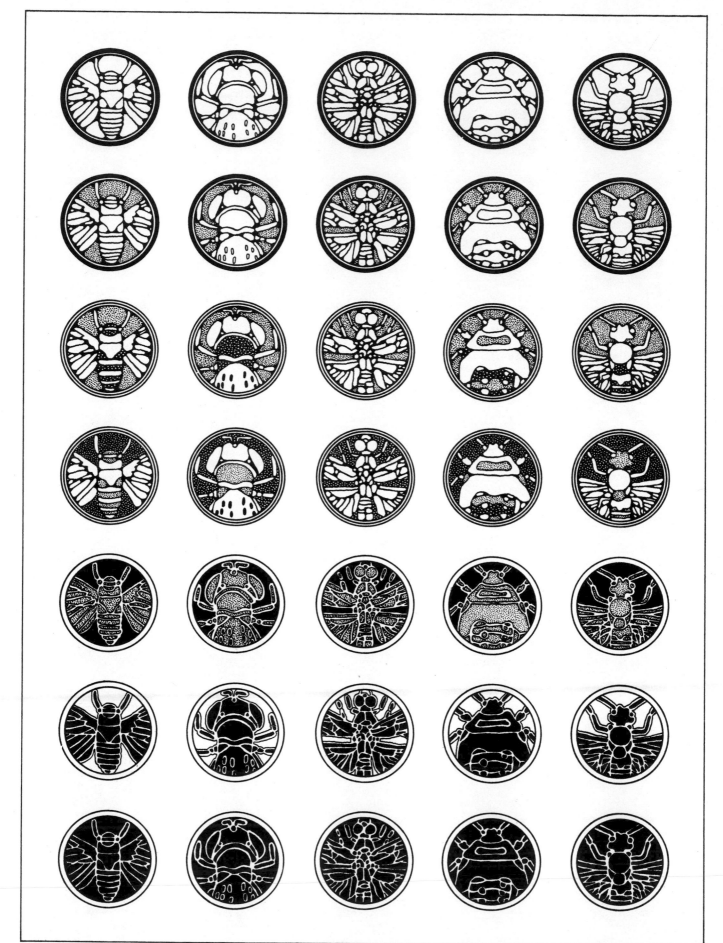

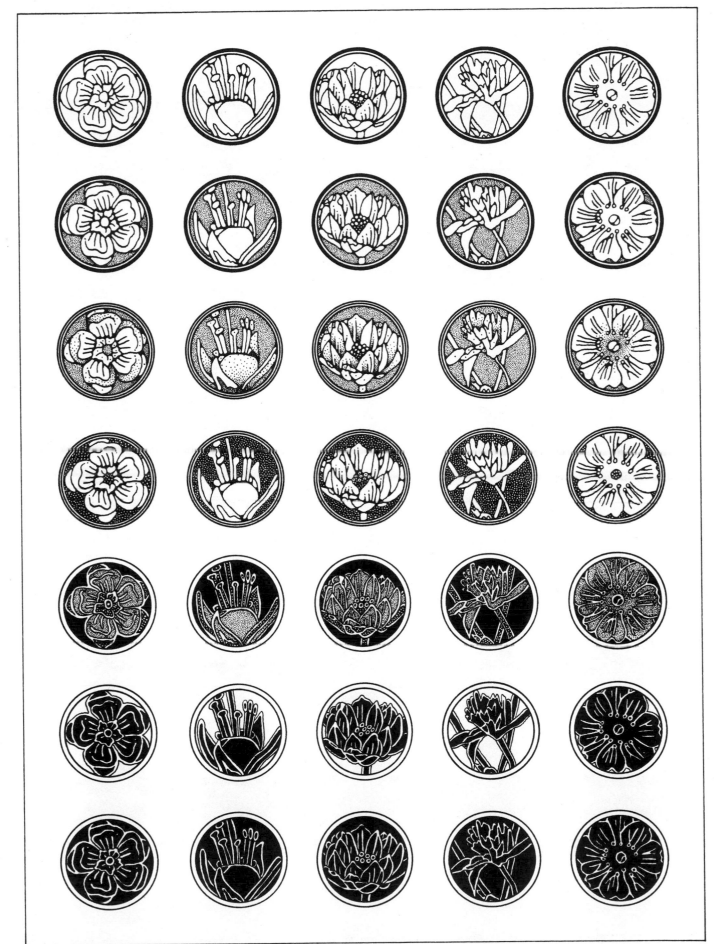

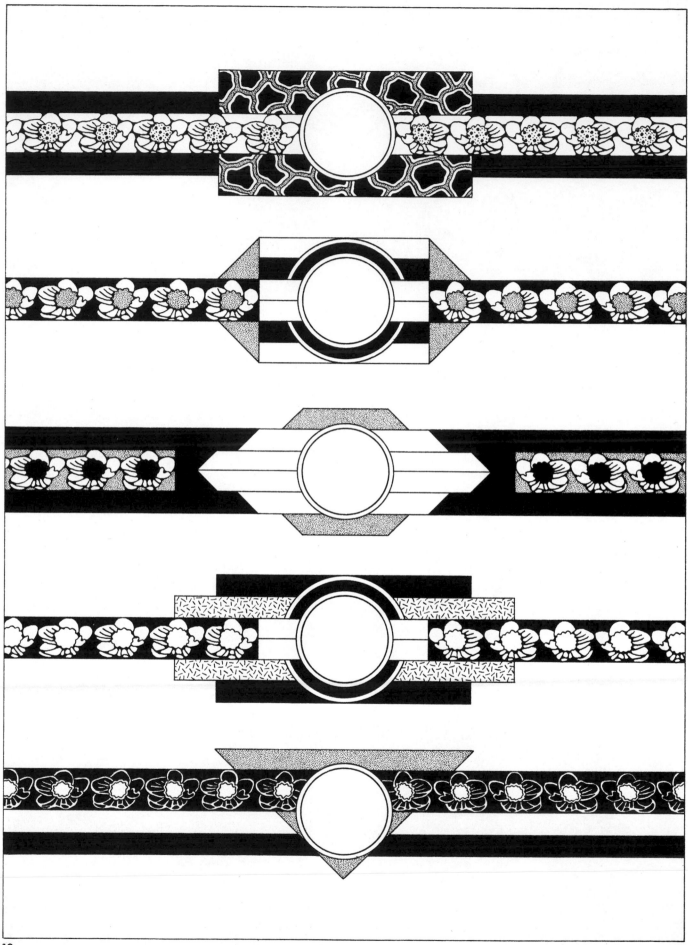

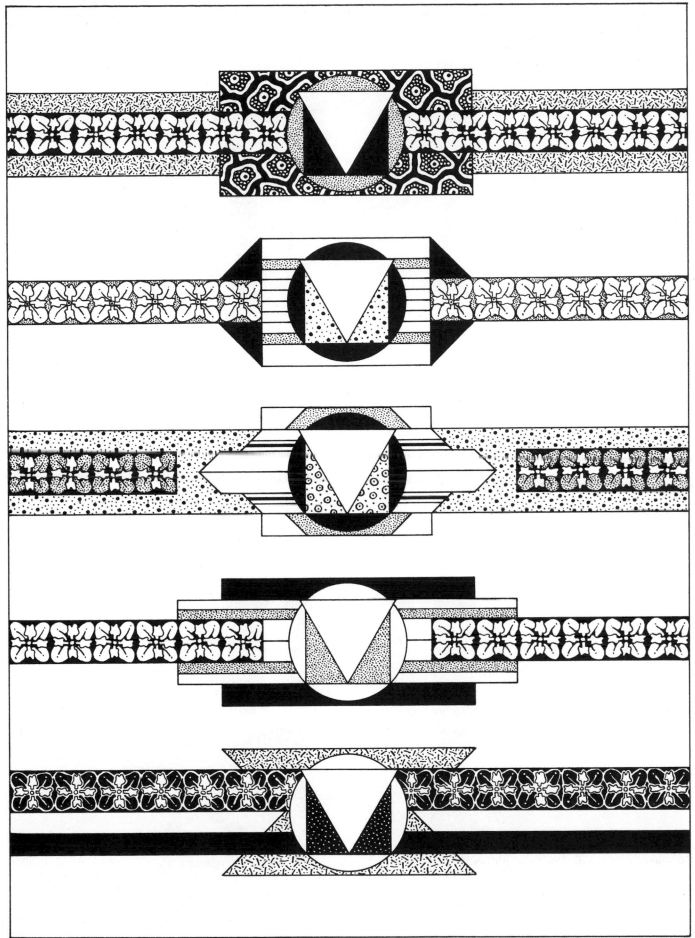

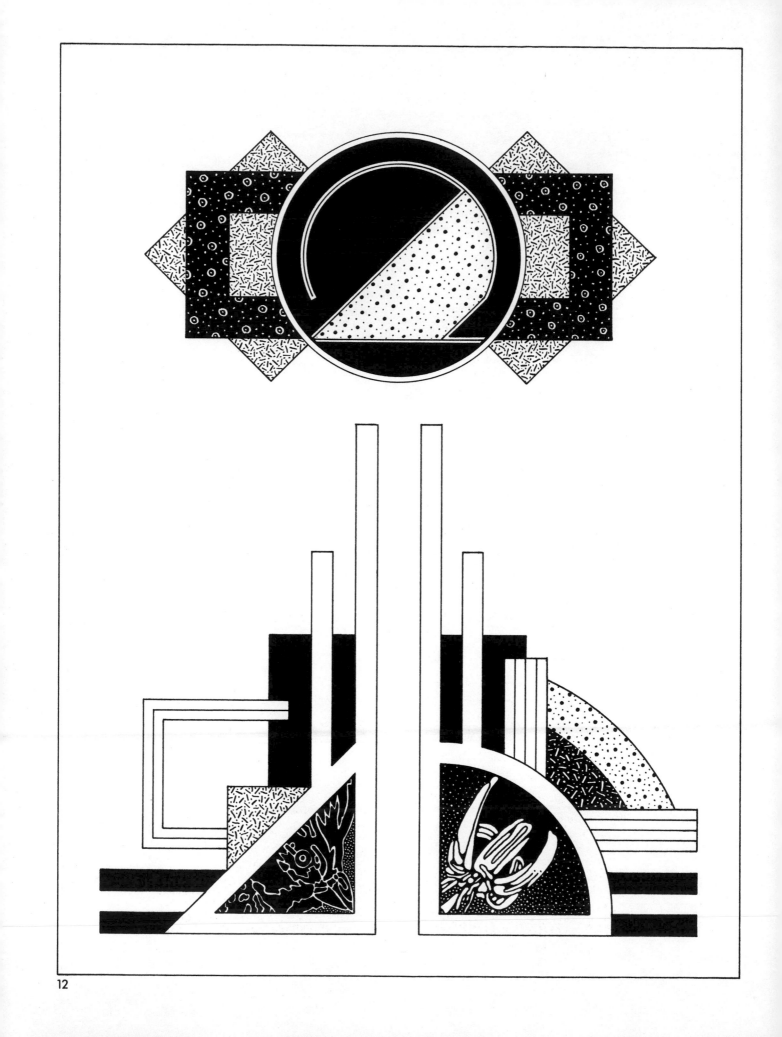

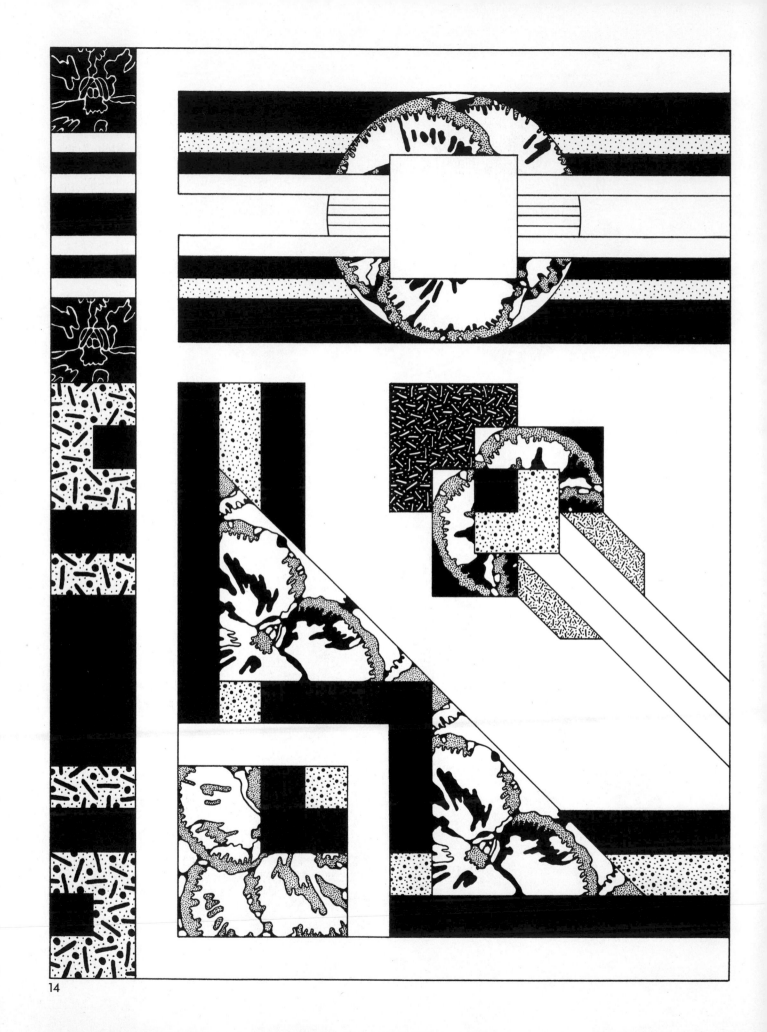

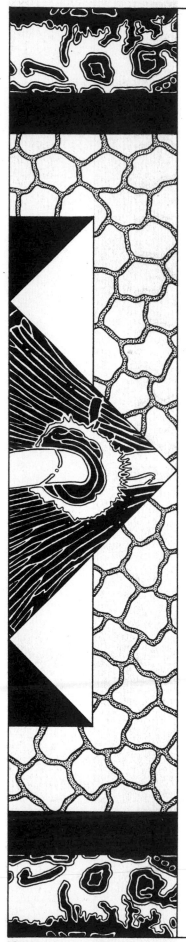

19

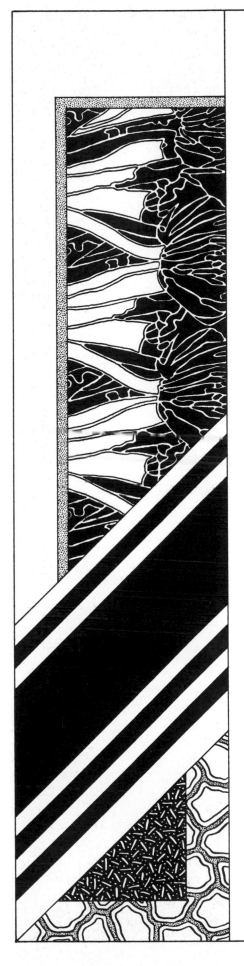

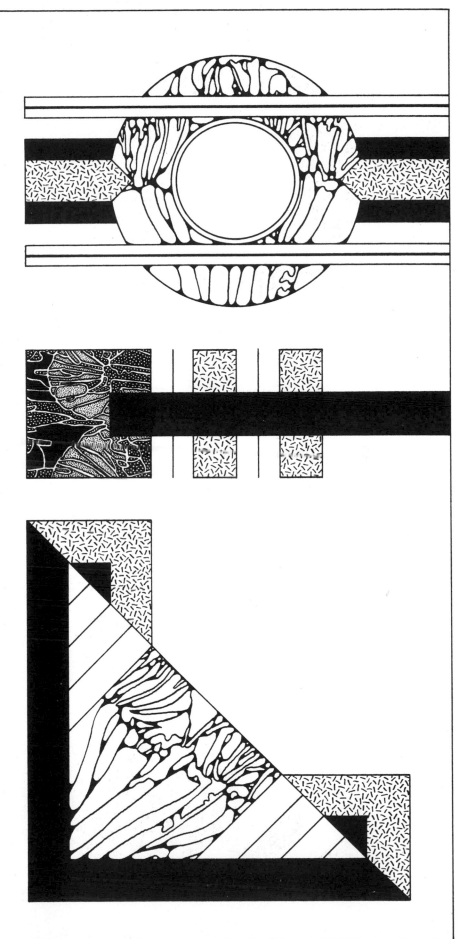

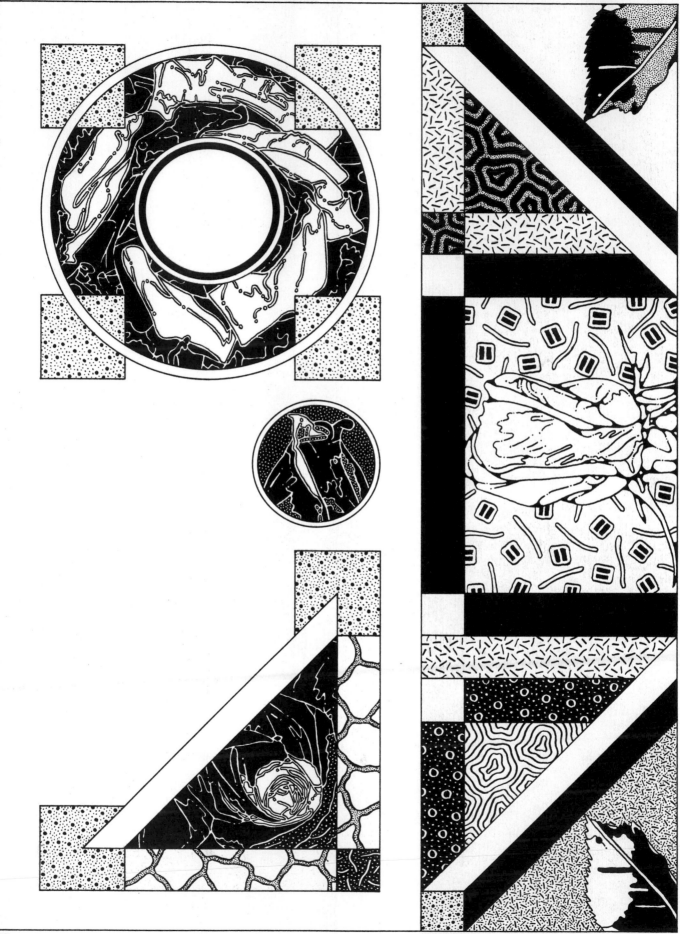

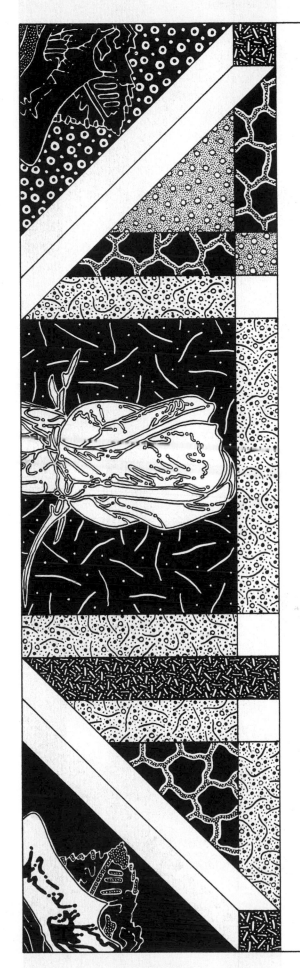
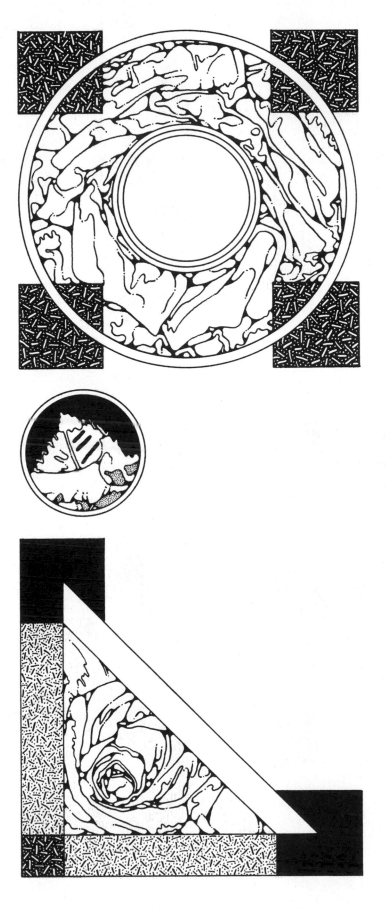

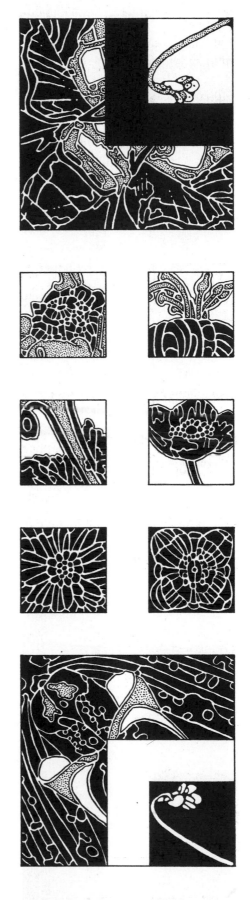

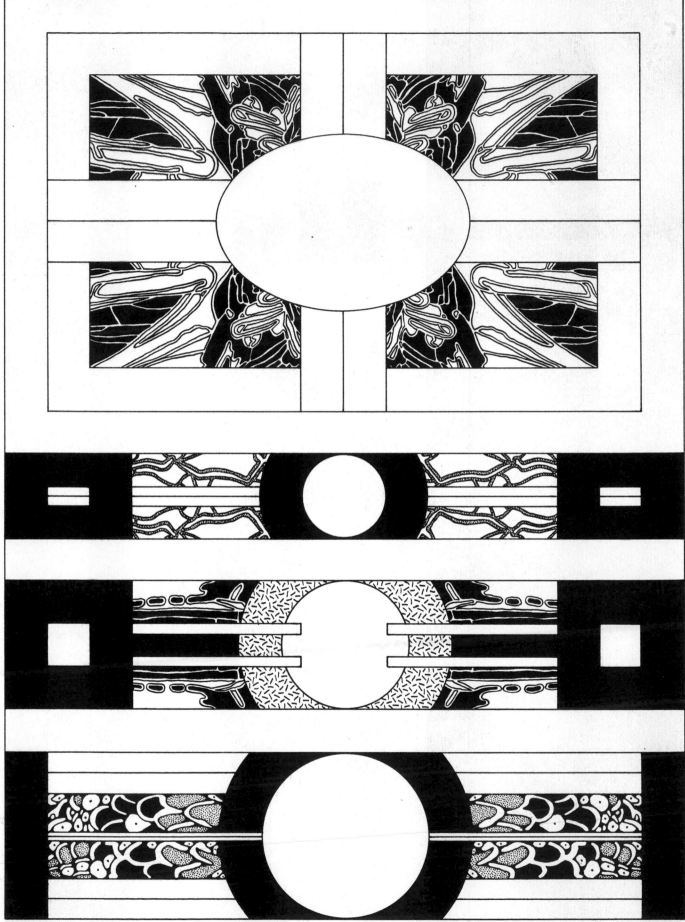

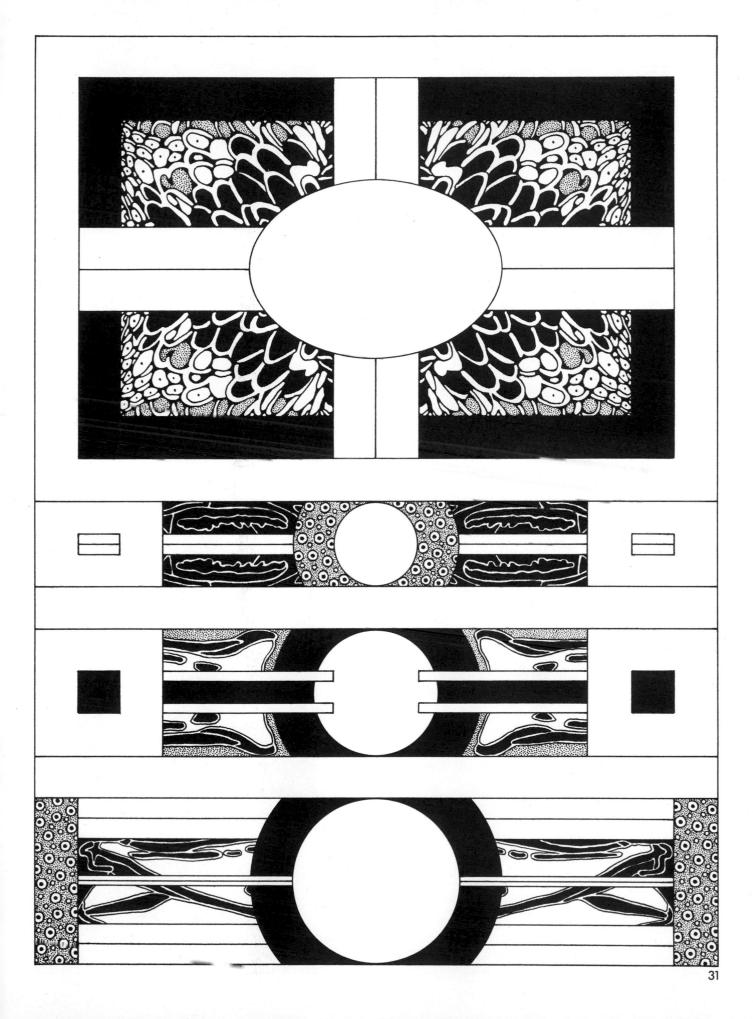

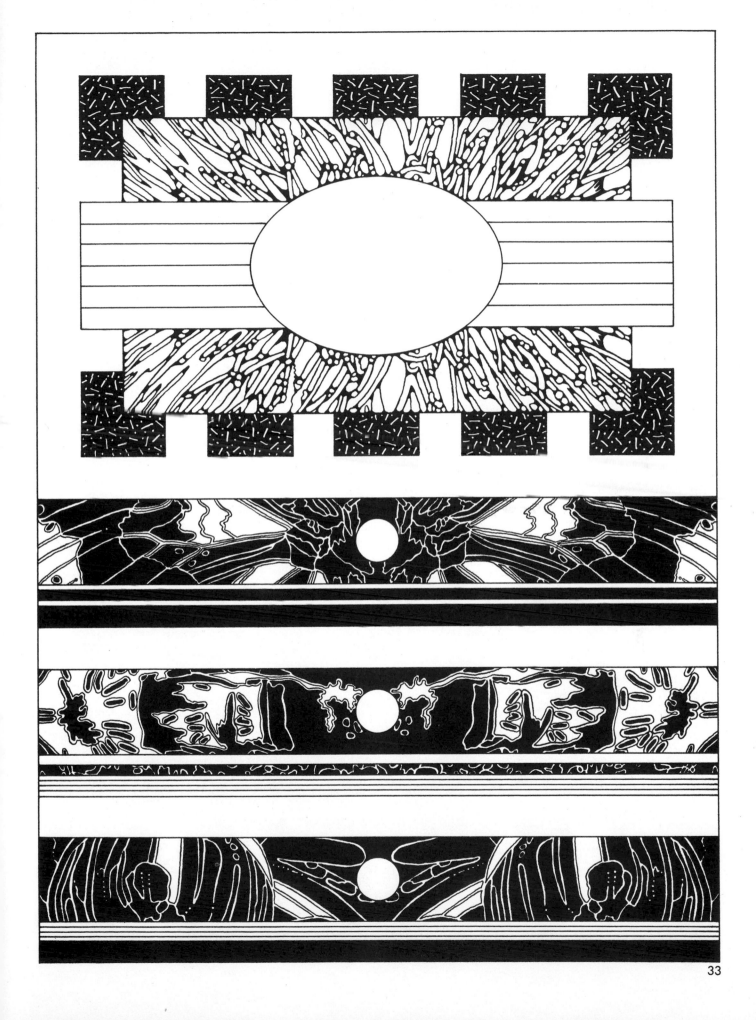

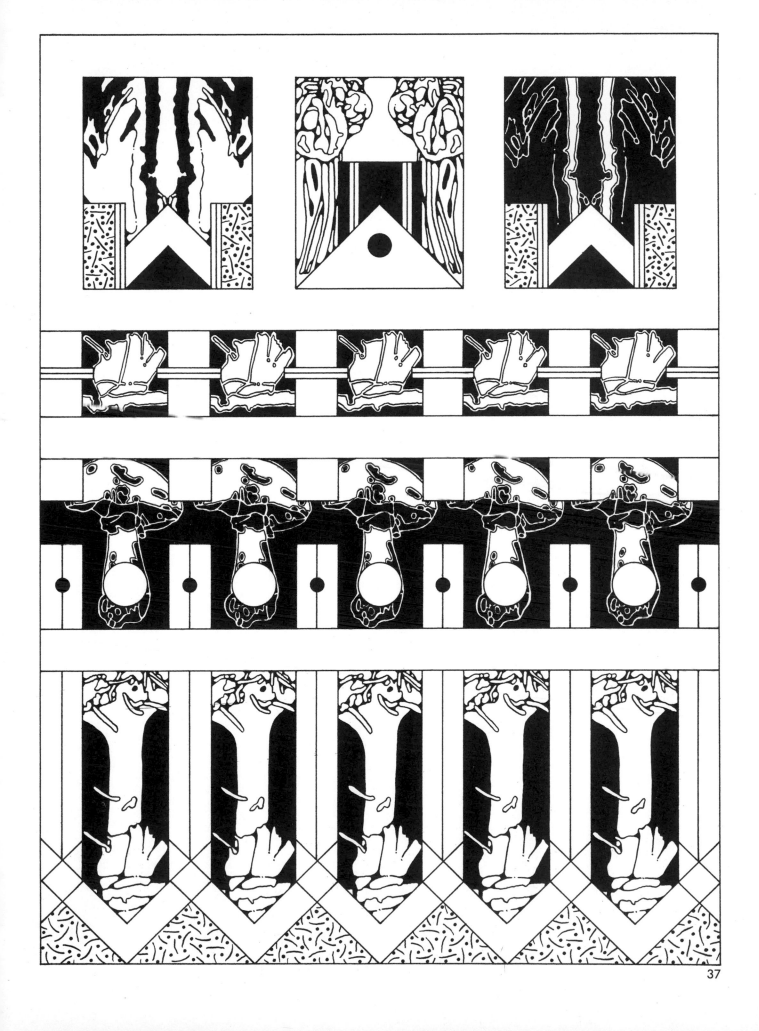

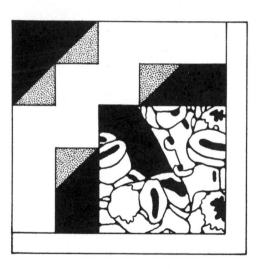

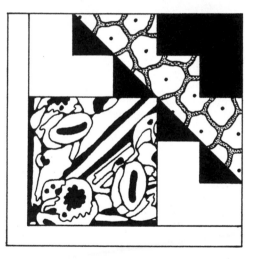

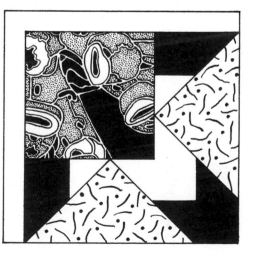

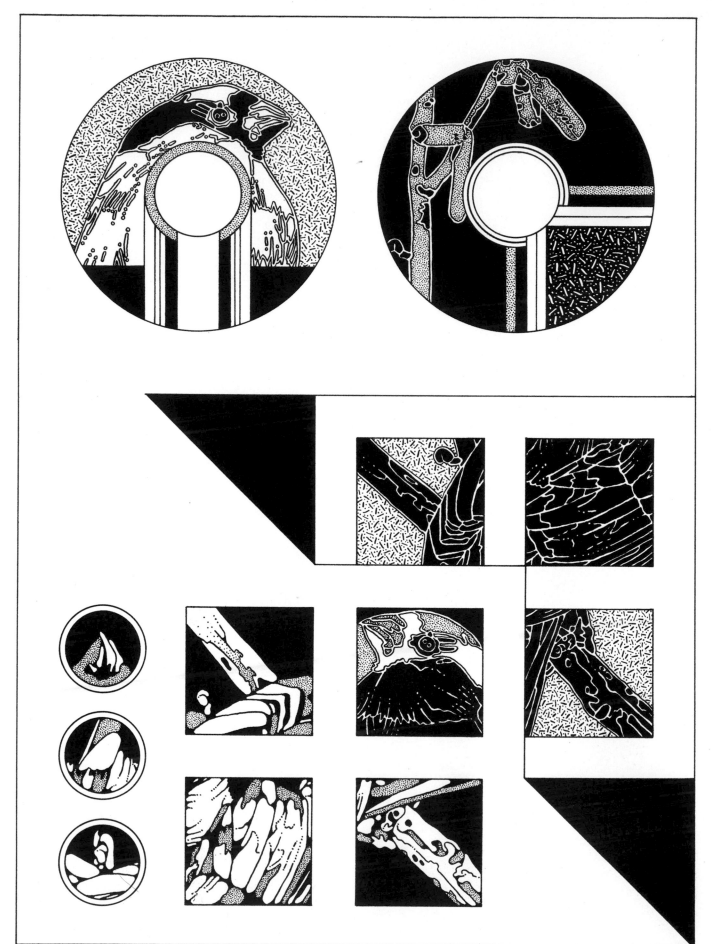

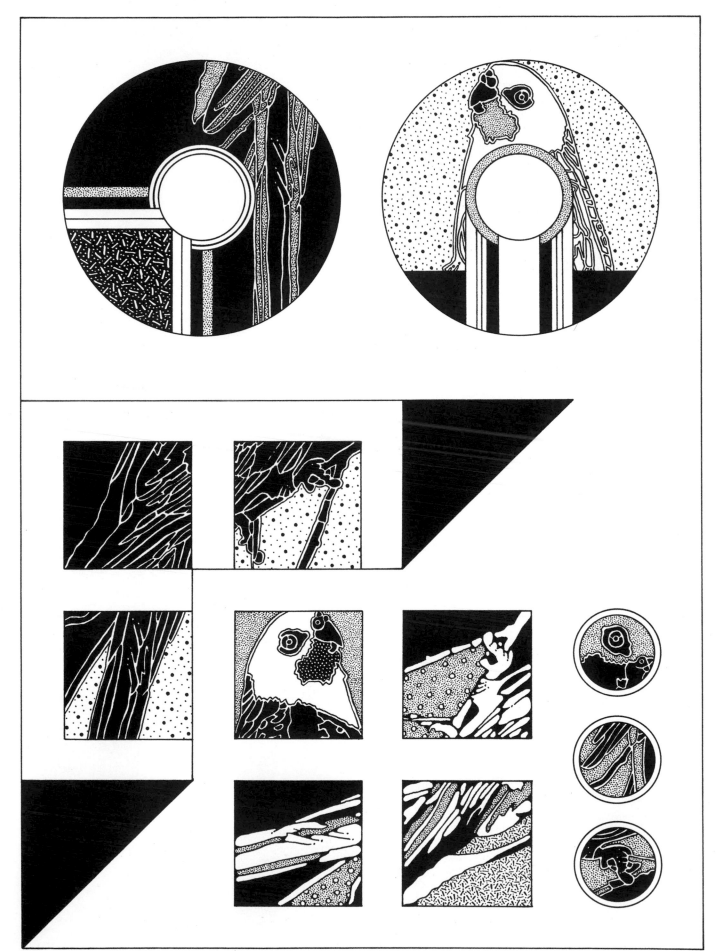

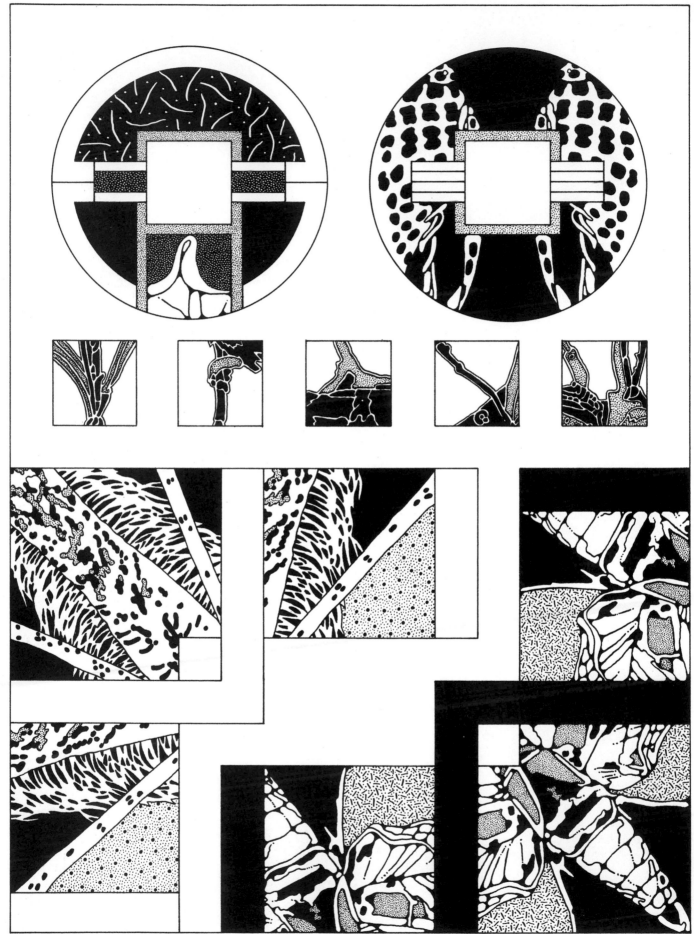

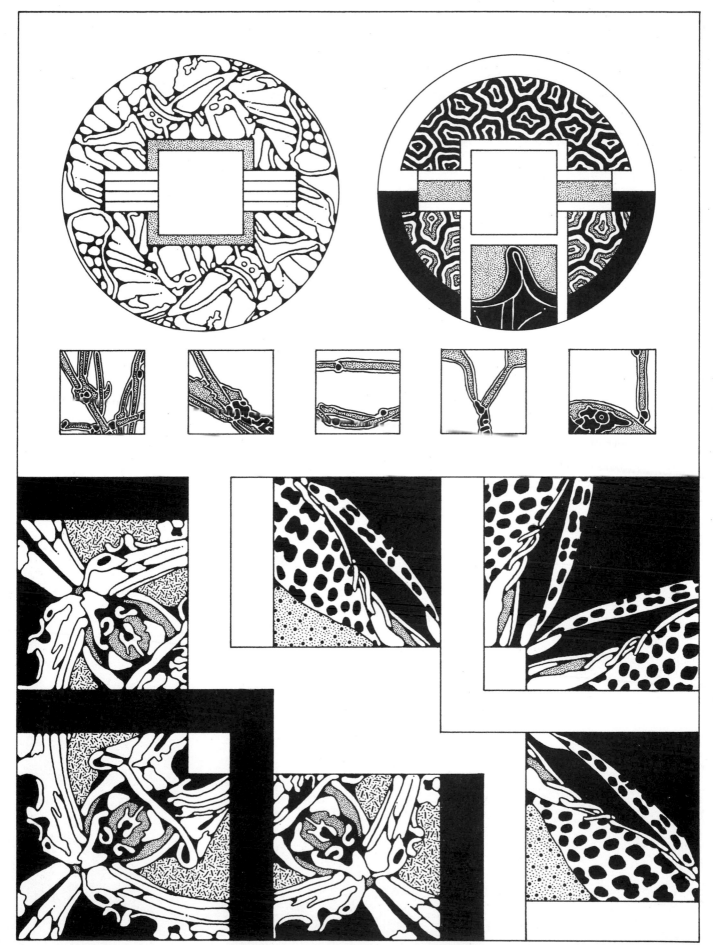

54

55

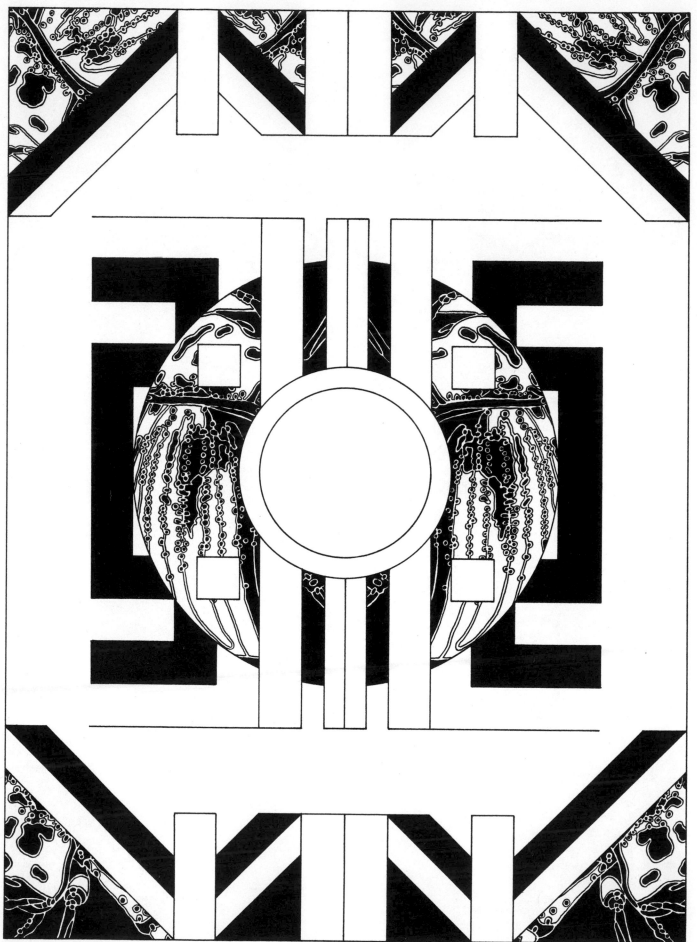

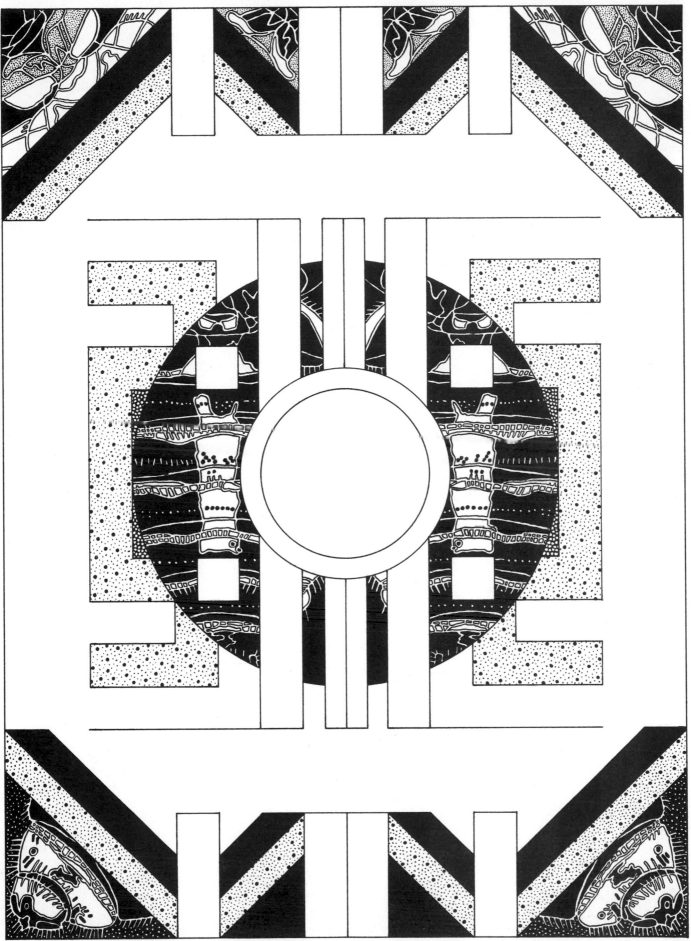